PENGUIN YOUNG RE

D0103033

At the Beach

by Alexa Andrews
illustrated by Candice Keimig
and with photographs

Penguin Young Readers
An Imprint of Penguin Group (USA) Inc.

In the Water

Fish live in the water.

Dolphins live in the water.

Sharks live in the water.

Whales live in the water.

Turtles live in the water.

Jellyfish live in the water.

Starfish live in the water.

Clams live in the water.

On the Sand

Shells are on the sand.

Beach balls are on the sand.

Crabs are on the sand.

Buckets are on the sand.

Towels are on the sand.

Sunglasses are on the sand.

Beach chairs are on the sand.

Surfboards are on the sand.

At the Beach

Umbrellas are at the beach.

Birds are at the beach.

Sand castles are at the beach.

Trees are at the beach.

Kites are at the beach.